The *Fantasy* of *Flowers*

The Fantasy of Flowers

by Boris Vallejo and Julie Bell

COURAGE
BOOKS

AN IMPRINT OF RUNNING PRESS
PHILADELPHIA • LONDON

© 2006 by Running Press
Photography © 2006 by Boris Vallejo and Julie Bell
All rights reserved under the Pan-American and International Copyright Conventions
Printed in China

9 8 7 6 5 4 3 2 1
Digit on the right indicates the number of this printing.

ISBN–13: 978-0-7624-2755-0
ISBN–10: 0-7624-2755-8
Library of Congress Control Number: 2005928384

Designed by Corinda Cook
Edited by Michael Tomolonis

This book may be ordered by mail from the publisher. *But try your bookstore first!*

Published by Courage Books, an imprint of
Running Press Book Publishers
125 South Twenty-second Street
Philadelphia, Pennsylvania 19103-4399

Visit us on the web!
www.runningpress.com

Contents

Introduction

We bought our first digital camera a few years ago and discovered a world of instant gratification. We no longer had to develop film and spend long hours in the darkroom printing black and white pictures as a reference for our paintings. Later, we purchased a close-up lens and another window opened. Minute things that had been ignored in nature became beautiful, intricate sources of wonder and joyful fun. Color, our most beloved friend throughout our artistic careers, became easily available at home with our switch to digital photography.

We are artists by profession. We talk with pictures. When we paint, we attempt to create Fantasy Art in imitation of Nature. We also love photography. When we take pictures, we attempt to portray the Fantasy of Nature in imitation of Art.

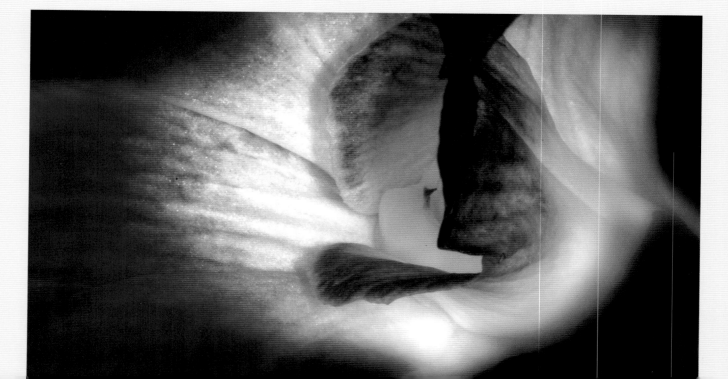

We have always been drawn to the art of the Art Nouveau period which is known for its organic, floral motifs. The furrows of a dragon's fins, the long flowing hair of a warrior princess, and the folds of a hero's flying cape all have their roots within the design of flowers.

Few things in nature are as versatile as flowers. You can look at them at a distance and be mesmerized by the richness and variety of colors, or you can look at them at close range and be amazed by the delicacy of their sometimes abstract and symmetrical design. Then again you can look at them closer and a new universe unfolds to the eye of the camera and then your own.

We are familiar with the quotes spread though the book that you are holding in your hand, and we are honored to be in the company of so many great thinkers who have also been inspired by the beauty of flowers. Getting lost in the vivid colors and winding shapes of flowers can bring us to the point of breathlessness.

We are using the photographs of the flowers in the same way we use paint to illustrate a little story, to simply revel in the beauty in front of us, and even to create a harmonious graphic design. We think of light and shadow and we think of composition. It is quite unlikely that anybody looking at our pictures will see a flower the same way that they would see it on their gardens or sitting at table at a restaurant. In fact, in shooting a flower we like to see the flower from a more intimate point of view.

We're not gardeners or experts on flowers in any way, and this fact gives us a different perspective. We see them not by variety, but purely by their design, shape, color, texture, transparency, and luminescence.

Some of the flowers are shown at different stages of their life cycle, some before they are fully in bloom, and some after they have mostly withered and decayed. The beauty of nature is clear in all of its stages and forms.

And so, we present to you a selection of pictures of our beautiful friends. We love them all.

Boris Vallejo and Julie Bell

Summer, 2005

Understanding

I know of no other genus whose plants
flower out-of-doors every day of the year.
I know of no other genus with one or more
species coming into bloom or growth,
peaking or going dormant at every season.

Nancy Goodwin

20th-century American writer

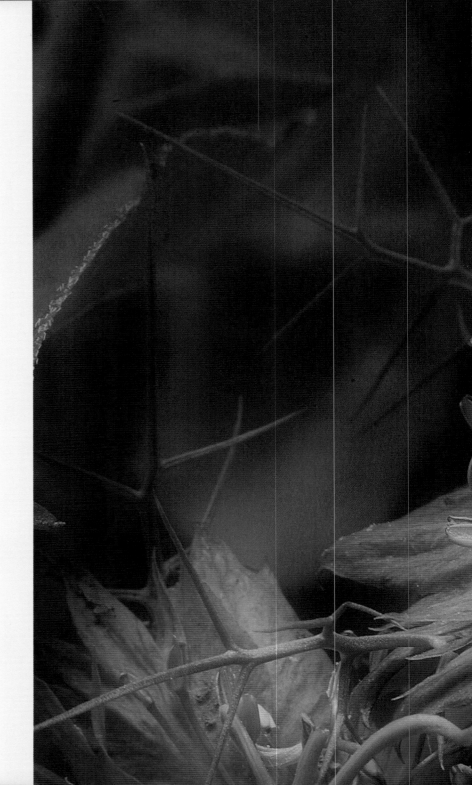

If you pass by
the color
purple in a
field and
don't notice it,
God gets
real pissed off.

Alice Walker (b. 1944)

American writer

I didn't know what narcissism was until I beheld my own narcissus.

Charles Kuralt (1934–1997)

American journalist

Observe this dew-drenched rose of Tyrian gardens

A rose today. But you will ask in vain

Tomorrow what it is; and yesterday

It was the dust, the sunshine, and the rains.

Christina Rosetti (1830–1894)

English poet

The actual flower is the plant's highest fulfillment,
and are not here exclusively for herbaria,
county floras and plant geography:
they are here first of all for delight.

John Ruskin (1819–1900)

English poet, philosopher

Forsythia is pure joy.

There is not an ounce, not a glimmer of sadness

or even knowledge in forsythia.

Pure, undiluted, untouched joy.

Anne Morrow Lindbergh (1906–2001)

American writer

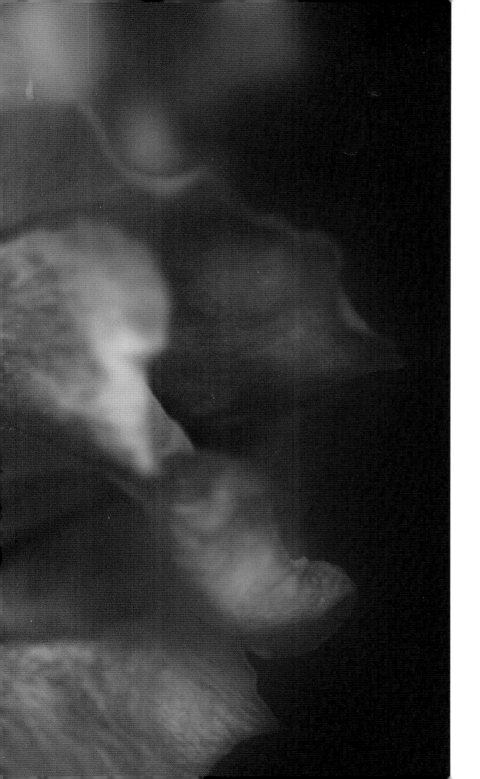

It will never
rain roses.
When we
want to have
more roses,
we must plant
more roses.

George Eliot (1819–1880)

English poet

One of the most attractive things about the flowers is their beautiful reserve.

Henry David Thoreau (1817–1862)

American author

Science, or para-science, tells us that geraniums bloom better if they are spoken to. But a kind word every now and then is really quite enough. Too much attention, like too much feeding, and weeding and hoeing, inhibits and embarrasses them.

Victoria Glendinning (b. 1937)

English writer

18

A rose is a rose is a rose.

Gertrude Stein (1874–1946)

American writer

I have a garden of my own,
But so with roses overgrown,
And lilies, that you would it
guess to be a little wilderness.

Andrew Marvell (1621–1678)

English poet

A flowerless room is a soulless room,
to my way of thinking;
but even a solitary little vase of a
living flower may redeem it.

Vita Sackville–West (1892–1962)

English writer

Hope and Joy

Where flowers bloom
so does hope.

Lady Bird Johnson (b. 1912)

First Lady

I will be the gladdest thing under the sun!
I will touch a hundred flowers and not pick one.

Edna St. Vincent Millay (1892–1950)

American poet

Flowers are the sweetest
things God ever made
and forgot to put a soul into.

Henry Ward Beecher (1813–1887)

American writer

All the flowers of all the tomorrows are in the seeds of today.

Indian proverb

In the hope of reaching the moon
men fail to see the flowers that
blossom at their feet.

Albert Schweitzer (1875–1965)

German theologian, musician, philosopher

Every flower about a house certifies to the refinement of somebody. Every vine climbing and blossoming tells of love and joy.

Robert G. Ingersoll (1833–1899)

American political leader

The Amen! of nature is always a flower.

Oliver Wendell Holmes (1809–1894)

American poet

The nature of this flower is to bloom.

Alice Walker (b. 1944)

American writer

In this world we walk on the
roof of hell gazing at flowers.

Issa (1763–1827)

Japanese haiku poet

When
words
escape,
flowers
speak.

Bruce W. Currie (b. 1911)

American poet

Beauty and Imagination

Art is the unceasing effort to compete with the beauty of flowers—and never succeeding.

Marc Chagall (1887–1985)

Russian-born French artist and writer

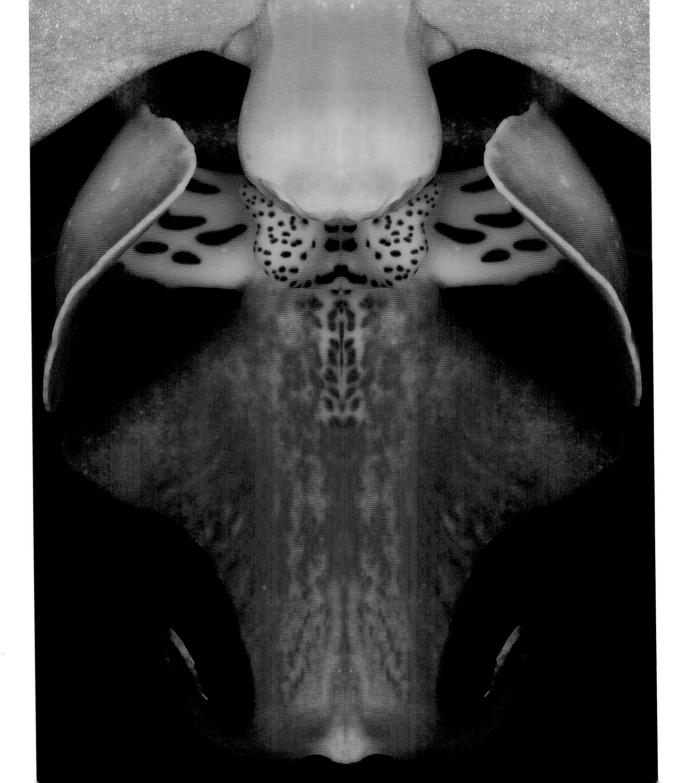

*Each flower is a soul
opening out to nature.*

Gerald De Nerval (1808–1855)

French symbolist writer

If seeds in the black earth can
turn into such beautiful roses,
what might not the heart
of man become in its long
journey toward the stars?

G. K. Chesterton (1874–1936)

English writer

Flowers are not made
by singing "Oh, how beautiful,"
and sitting in the shade.

Rudyard Kipling (1865–1936)

English poet

I perhaps
owe having
become
a painter
to flowers.

Claude Monet (1840–1926)

French painter

Often the prickly thorn produces tender roses.

Ovid (43 B.C.–A.D. 17)

Roman poet

As well as
any bloom
upon a flower
I like the
dust on the
nettles,
never lost
except to
prove the
sweetness
of a shower.

Edward Thomas (1878–1917)

English poet

Flowers bring
to a liberal and
gentlemanly
mind the
remembrance
of honest,
comeliness
and all kinds
of virtues.

John Gerard (1922–1986)

English novelist

Who would have thought it possible that a tiny little flower could preoccupy a person so completely that there simply wasn't room for any other thought. . .

Sophie Scholl (1921–1943)

German artist

I was not looking now at an
unusual flower arrangement.
I was seeing what Adam
had seen on the morning
of his creation—the miracle,
moment by moment,
of naked existence.

Aldous Huxley (1894–1963)

English writer

To analyze the charms of flowers is like dissecting music;

it is one of those things which it is far better to enjoy,

than to attempt to fully understand.

Henry T. Tuckerman (1813–1871)

American essayist

Be like the flower,
turn your faces to the sun.

Kahlil Gibran (1883–1931)

Lebanese poet

Flowers are beautiful hieroglyphics of nature, with which she indicates how much she loves us.

Johann Wolfgang von Goethe (1749–1832)

German poet

Arranging a bowl of flowers in the morning can give a sense of quiet in a crowded day—like writing a poem, or saying a prayer.

Anne Morrow Lindbergh (1906–2001)

American poet, aviator

Friendship

To pick a flower is so much more satisfying
than just observing it, or photographing it . . .
so in later years, I have grown in my garden
as many flowers as possible for children to pick.

Anne Scott-James (b. 1913)

American journalist

True friendship is like a rose: we don't realize its beauty until it fades.

Evelyn Loeb

20th-century German author

54

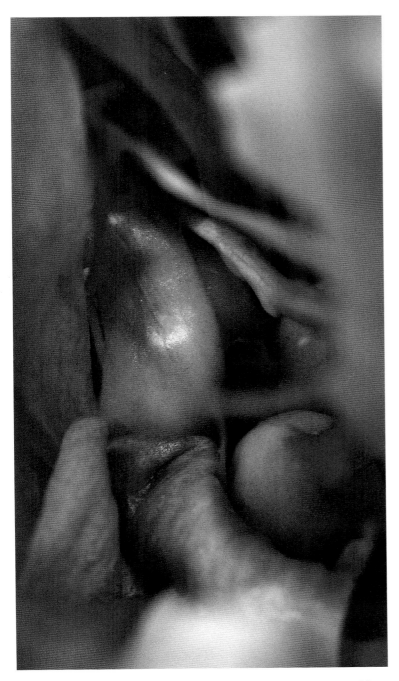

In the cherry blossom's shade there's no such thing as a stranger.

Issa (1763–1827)

Japanese haiku poet

When you take a flower in your hand and really look at it, it's your world for the moment. I want to give that world to someone else. Most people in the city rush around so, they have no time to look at a flower. I want them to see it whether they want to or not.

Georgia O'Keeffe (1887–1985)

American artist

In joy or sadness, flowers are our constant friends.

Kazuko Okakura

20th-century Japanese art historian

I didn't know the names of the flowers—now my garden is gone.

Allen Ginsberg (1926–1997)

American poet

And 'tis my
faith
that every
flower
Enjoys the
air it
breathes.

William Wordsworth (1770–1850)

English poet

Sensations

The Earth Laughs in Flowers.

Ralph Waldo Emerson (1803–1882)

American writer

Perfumes are the feelings of flowers.

Heinrich Heine (1797–1856)

German poet

A flower's fragrance declares to all the world that it is fertile, available, and desirable, its sex organs oozing with nectar . . . we inhale its ardent aroma and, no matter what our ages, we feel young and nubile in a world aflame with desire.

Diane Ackerman (b. 1948)

American poet, author

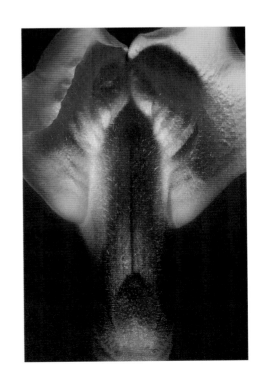

With a few flowers
in my garden,
half a dozen pictures
and some books,
I live without envy.

Lope de Vega (1562–1635)

Spanish playwright

The world is a rose; smell it
and pass it to your friends.

Persian proverb

The flower is the poetry of reproduction.
It is an example of
the eternal seductiveness of life.

Jean Giraudoux (1882–1944)

French novelist

Let us open our leaves like a flower, and be passive and receptive.

John Keats (1795–1821)

English poet

The gardens that make us happiest flourish because we have taken the time to make sure they feed our souls and fill a special place in our lives. Sometimes you have to think about what you really want from your garden . . . once the beds are laid out and the rose bushes planted.

Lindley Karstens (b. 1961)

American artist

Flowers are restful to look at.
They have neither emotions nor conflicts.

Sigmund Freud (1856–1939)

Austrian neurologist

Flowers never emit so
sweet and strong a fragrance
as before a storm.
When a storm approaches thee,
be as fragrant as
a sweet-smelling flower.

Jean Paul Richter (1763–1825)

German writer

The flowers take the tears of weeping night

And give them to the sun for the day's delight.

Joseph S. Cotter, Sr. (1861–1949)

American poet

Colors are
the smiles of
nature . . .
they are
her laughs,
as in flowers.

Leigh Hunt (1784–1859)

English writer

*flowers and plants are silent presences;
they nourish every sense except the ear.*

May Sarton (1912–1995)

Belgian-born American writer

People from a
planet without
flowers would
think we must
be mad with joy
the whole time
to have such
things about us.

Iris Murdoch (b. 1919)

Irish writer

Philosophy

Flowers are love's truest language.

Park Benjamin (1809–1864)

American journalist

There came a time when the risk to remain tight in the bud was more painful than the risk it took to blossom.

Anaïs Nin (1903–1977)

French writer

What's in a name?
That which we call a rose
by any other name
would smell as sweet.

William Shakespeare (1564–1616)

English playwright, poet

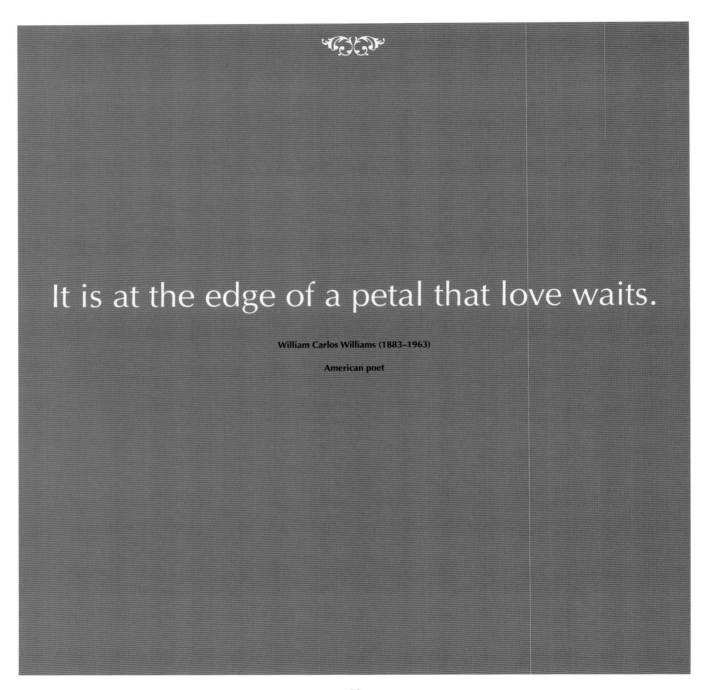

It is at the edge of a petal that love waits.

William Carlos Williams (1883–1963)

American poet

If there were nothing else to trouble us,
  the fate of the flowers would make us sad.

John Lancaster Spalding (1840–1916)

Catholic prelate

There are philosophies as varied as the flowers of the field, and some of them weeds and a few of them poisonous weeds. But none of them create the psychological conditions in which I first saw, or desired to see, the flower.

G. K. Chesterton (1874–1936)

English writer

He who is born with a silver spoon in his mouth is generally considered a fortunate person, but his good fortune is small compared to that of the happy mortal who enters this world with a passion for flowers in his soul.

Celia Thaxter (1835–1894)

American poet

The flower that
you spent time
to care for does
not grow while
the willow that
you accidentally
planted flourishes
and gives shade.

Chinese proverb

Little flower, but if I could understand,
what you are, root and all in all,
I should know what God and man is.

Alfred Tennyson (1809–1892)

English poet

From a thorn comes
a rose, and from
a rose comes a thorn.

Greek proverb

He who wants a rose must respect the thorn.

Persian proverb

The rose has thorns only for those who would gather it.

Chinese proverb

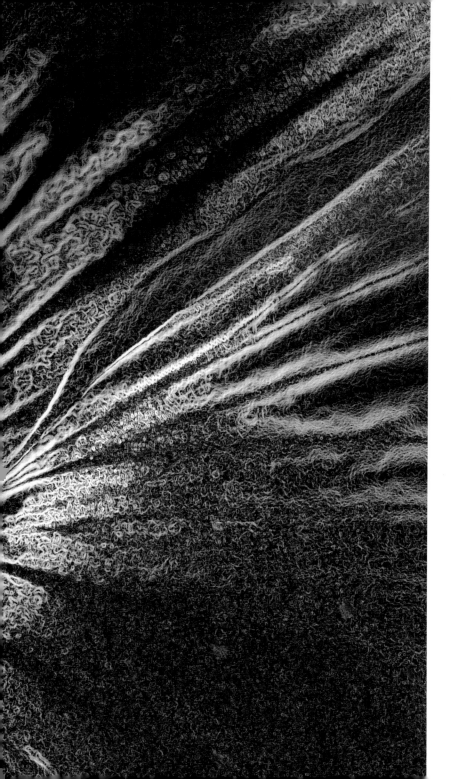

We can complain because rose bushes have thorns or rejoice because thorn bushes have roses.

Abraham Lincoln (1809–1865)

American president

Some people are always grumbling because roses have thorns. I am thankful that thorns have roses.

Alphonse Karr (1808–1890)

French novelist

flowers leave some of their fragrance in the hand that bestows them.

Chinese proverb

At dawn I asked the lotus, 'What is the meaning of life?' Slowly she opened her hand with nothing in it.

Debra Woolard Bender

20th-century American artist, poet

In the garden the door is always open into the "holy"—growth, birth, death. Every flower holds the whole mystery in its short cycle, and in the garden we are never far away from death, the fertilizing, good, creative death.

May Sarton (1912–1994)

Belgian writer